Crowdfinancing

Introducing a New Asset Class

Author: Douglas Slain

Table of Contents

Introduction 3
I.   What is crowdfunding? 5
II. Crowdfunding in Europe 17
III. Comparative Analysis of U.S. Crowdfunding Vehicles 21
About the author 24

Introduction

The JOBS Act's crowdfunding and private offering reforms in 2013 represent historically significant developments. Together with the deregulatory changes scheduled for 2014 these new reforms turn on its head the traditional orthodoxy embodied in the Securities Act of 1933.

The Securities Act of 1933 as administered by the Securities and Exchange Commission for the last 80 years has placed significant hurdles on startups and small businesses who want seed capital.

One objective of the JOBS Act was to enable the "small guy" to raise seed and capital through private placements, exempt from Federal or state registration. Accordingly, capital-seeking enterprises can now engage in heretofore prohibited general solicitation of individual and institutional investors with whom they do not have a prior relationship.

The JOBS Act's private offering reforms are already enabling market innovators to transform early stage capital formation, expanding opportunities for both accredited and non-accredited investors; they have democratized an area of investment from which ordinary investors have been excluded.

The market for private placements already eclipses that of public offerings. In 2012 companies raised more than

$900 billion in private placements, nearly four times the amount raised through public stock offerings, according to the SEC. Strikingly, private placements were only sold to under 250,000 investors in 2012. In 2014 and 2015, and beyond, this number will skyrocket. This monograph compares U.S. crowdfunding vehicles and platforms and summarizes what several EU countries are doing.

I. What is crowdfunding?

Crowdfunding is fundraising through securities offerings directed to the general public through the internet and other mass communications media. Under historic securities law, an offer made to the general public was considered a "public offering" that had to be registered with the SEC and registered or qualified with the securities regulator of each state in which the offering was conducted. This regulatory regime precluded crowdfunding by startups and private emerging growth companies.

The JOBS Act carved out a truly historic exemption for crowdfunding by adding a new transaction exemption in Section 4 of the Securities Act. Issuers and intermediaries are free to engage in crowdfunding activities that would otherwise be characterized as public offerings requiring registration under the Securities Act.

Funding platforms or intermediaries are increasingly making use of networking funding portals to attract and organize communities of angel investors.

1. Are all issuers eligible to rely on the crowdfunding exemption?

<u>No.</u>

The crowdfunding exemption is not available to foreign issuers, SEC-reporting issuers and certain investment companies. The exemption excludes from eligibility an issuer not organized under the laws of a state or territory of the United States or the District of Columbia; or is subject to reporting requirements pursuant to Section 13 or 15(d) of the Securities Exchange Act of 1934; or is an investment company, as defined in Section 3 of the Investment Company Act of 1940; or is excluded from the definition of investment company by Section 3(b) or Section 3(c) of the Investment Company Act of 1940.

Publicly traded companies may not engage in crowdfunding exempt offerings. Similarly, a private fund excluded from regulation as an investment company under Section 3(c)(1) or 3(c)(7) of the Investment Company Act (whether formed as a pool investment vehicle or a conduit formed for investment in a particular issuer) also may not rely on the crowdfunding exemption.

The SEC has the rulemaking authority to exclude from eligibility other companies as it may determine appropriate.

2. Can issuers engage in unrestricted general solicitation and advertising with crowdfunding exempt offerings?

No.

While issuers are free to introduce the general public to an online platform through which the securities are discussed, they may not actually directly offer the securities themselves. Instead, they must direct prospective investors to intermediaries or funding portals. This is meant to preclude use of making offerings via blast emails and similar communications.

Registered intermediaries, on the other hand, are allowed to promote crowdfunding offerings.

3. Are issuers required to conduct crowdfunding exempt offerings through intermediaries or broker-dealers?

Yes.

Crowdfunding offerings may not be conducted by an issuer directly, using its website or otherwise. Crowdfunding offerings must be conducted through funding portals or through a licensed broker-dealer network.

4. How much capital can an issuer raise through the Title III crowdfunding exemption?

Issuers can sell up to $1,000,000 aggregate amount of securities, sold through crowdfunding exempt offerings, during any 12 month period.

5. Does the crowdfunding exemption impose limits on the number of investors who can invest?

<u>No.</u>

There is no limit on the number of investors who can invest. Further, investors who become security holders through crowdfunding exempt offerings are excluded when calculating the number of record holders under Section 12(g) of the Securities Exchange Act.

6. Does the crowdfunding exemption impose limits on how much any investor can invest?

<u>Yes.</u>

The crowdfunding exemption limits how much an investor may invest based on the investor's annual income or net worth and includes all exempt investments made in the 12-month period preceding the investment in question. The limits are:

1. for investors with either an annual income or net worth less than $100,000, the amount invested may not exceed the greater of $2,000 or 5% of the investor's annual income or net worth; and 2) for investors with either an annual income or net worth of at least $100,000, the amount invested may not exceed 10% of the investor's annual income or net worth up to a $100,000 maximum aggregate amount.

The crowdfunding exemption also imposes a requirement on intermediaries to make such efforts as the SEC may determine appropriate to ensure that no investor in the prescribed preceding 12-month period has purchased crowdfunding exempt securities from all issuers that exceed the individual investment limits described above.

7. What is a funding portal within the meaning of new Rule 506?

Section 3(a) (80) of the Securities Act, added by the JOBS Act, defines a funding portal as anyone engaged in the business of effecting transactions in securities for the account of others, solely pursuant to the crowdfunding exemption contained in Section 4(a) (6) of the Securities Act.

A funding portal is not permitted to:
- offer investment advice or recommendations
- compensate employees, agents, or other persons for such solicitation or based on the sale of securities displayed or referenced on its website or portal;
- hold, manage, possess, or otherwise handle investor funds or securities; or
- engage in such other activities as the SEC may determine appropriate.

Brokers or dealers operating in the over-the-counter market for PIPRs (Private Issuers Publicly Raising) must register under the Securities Exchange Act and become a member of a registered securities association or join a self-regulatory organization. New Section 3(h) of the Securities Exchange Act requires the SEC to exempt a registered

funding portal from the requirement to register as a broker or dealer, provided that the funding portal:
- remains subject to the examination, enforcement, and other rulemaking authority of the SEC;
- is a member of a national securities association registered under Section 15A of the Securities Exchange Act (such as FINRA or an association organized by the crowdfunding industry); and
- is subject to such other requirements under this title as the SEC may determine.

8. What liabilities are occasioned by violations of law with exempt offerings?

Investors in crowdfunding offerings may institute actions for rescission or damages. As is the case with liability under Section 12(a) (2) of the Securities Act for public offerings, defendants can defeat liability if they can demonstrate an adequate due diligence defense, i.e., that they have conducted a reasonable investigation as has been developed by the federal courts in their interpretation of Section 12(a) (2) of the Securities Act.

Section 4A(c) (3) of Securities Act contains an expansive definition of the term "issuer" for purposes of the liability provisions. The term "issuer" includes any person who is a director or partner of the issuer, and the principal executive officer or officers, principal financial officer, and controller or principal accounting officer of the issuer (and any person occupying a similar status or performing a similar function) that offers or sells a security in a crowdfunding exempt offering, and any person who offers or sells the security in such offering.

Since crowdfunding offerings are expressly exempt from registration, issuers and their intermediaries will not be subject to liability under Section 11 of the Securities Act for any disclosure defects contained in any registration statement. As is the case with any securities transaction, crowdfunding exempt offerings are subject to the general anti-fraud provisions of Section 10(b) of the Securities Exchange Act and Rule 10b-5 thereunder.

9. How are investors in crowdfunding offerings treated for purposes of calculating the number of record holders triggering registration under Section 12(g) of the Securities Exchange Act?

Section 12(g) of the Securities Exchange Act in its form prior to the enactment of the JOBS Act mandates that a private issuer with 500 or more shareholders and more than $10 million in assets register as public reporting issuer and comply with ongoing SEC periodic reporting requirements. As has was the case with Facebook remaining a private company, the 500 holder threshold has been a burden on many private enterprises.

The crowdfunding reforms also amend Section 12(g) to require the SEC to exempt from Section 12(g), conditionally or unconditionally, securities acquired in crowdfunding exempt offerings.

10. Can state securities commissioners regulate rowdfunding offerings?

State blue sky registration, documentation and offering requirements that would otherwise apply to crowdfunding exempt offerings are preempted. The JOBS Act amends Section 18(b)(4) of the Securities Act to add to the list of covered securities for which preemption applies securities that are the subject of crowdfunding offerings exempt under Section 4(a)(6) of the Securities Act.

However, this amendment does not affect any state's enforcement authority over an issuer, broker, dealer, or funding portal for fraud or deceit or unlawful conduct in crowdfunding exempt offerings. There will be a filing and fee requirement with the securities regulator of the state in which the issuer maintains its principal place of business or in which purchasers of 50% or greater of the aggregate amount of the securities issued are residents.

In addition, the JOBS Act preempts state blue sky regulation of registered funding portals, except that the state where the funding portal maintains its principal place of business will retain enforcement and examination authority.

11. What resale restrictions apply to securities acquired in crowdfunding exempt offerings?

Securities sold in crowdfunding exempt offerings are not transferable by the purchaser for a one-year period beginning on the date of purchase, except such securities may be transferred:

- to the issuer,
- to an accredited investor,
- as part of an offering registered with the SEC; or
- to a member of the purchaser's family or the equivalent, or in connection with the purchaser's death or divorce or other similar circumstance, in the discretion of the SEC.

12. How do the private offering reforms expand opportunities for capital formation aside from the Regulation D private offering exemption?

Since its adoption in the 1980s, a majority of small businesses have relied on Regulation D under the Securities Act to raise debt and equity capital in U.S. private capital markets. Regulation D provides a non-exclusive safe harbor from registration of the offering with the SEC. Rule 506 of Regulation D permits offerings to an unlimited number of accredited investors in an unlimited dollar amount, provided that the issuers comply with the conditions set forth in the regulation. One key condition prohibits the issuer or any person acting on its behalf from offering or selling securities by any form of general solicitation or

general advertising, including, but not limited to:

(i) any advertisement, article, or other published or broadcast communication or

(ii) (ii) any seminar or meeting whose attendees have been invited by general solicitation or advertising. This prohibition on general solicitation also implicates private offerings conducted in reliance on Rule 144A under the Securities Act

Market participants have advocated to the SEC for well over a decade that the prohibition on general solicitation be removed provided that the ultimate sales are made to accredited investors. With implementation of the JOBS Act, this is now the law.

13. What is an issuer?

Section 4A(c) (3) of Securities Act contains an expansive definition of the term "issuer" for purposes of establishing liability. The term "issuer" includes any person who is a director or partner of the issuer, and the principal executive officer or officers, principal financial officer, and controller or principal accounting officer of the issuer (and any person occupying a similar status or performing a similar function) that offers or sells a security in a crowdfunding exempt offering. Since crowdfunding offerings are expressly exempt from registration, issuers and intermediaries will not be subject to liability under Section 11 of the Securities Act for any disclosure defects contained in any registration statements. As is the case with any securities transaction, crowdfunding exempt offerings will be subject to the general anti-fraud provisions of Section 10(b) of the Securities Exchange Act and Rule 10b-5 thereunder.

II. Crowdfunding in Europe

Country	Securities crowdfunding	Current requirements/ limitations	Crowdfunding Regulation status
France	Allowed only if platforms are licensed as financial investment advisers or monitored by the French banking monopoly (lending platforms).	Very high capital requirements for the platforms- Issuer can promote its capital offer up to only 149 investors	Consultation period for proposed legislation, that would create a new category of financial adviser for crowdfunding portals and remove the public promotion limit.
Germany	Allowed only if platforms have a license from BaFin. However, if the platform is only brokering silent partnerships, it does not need a license.	Threshold of 100.000€ offering within 12 months per issuer.	

17

Italy	Equity CF platforms need to register with CONSOB. Lending platforms need to be authorized by the Bank of Italy.	Only "innovative start-ups" can use equity CF- Threshold of €5m per issuer-5% of capital offered shall be subscribed by a professional investor.	CONSOB released regulations allowing retail investors to invest through equity crowdfunding.
The Netherlands	Platforms are considered investment firms, thus they require a license under the Dutch Financial Supervision Act.	Securities CF: Threshold:€2,5mln within 12 months per issuer	
Portugal	Difficult to implement, due to lack of regulation. It will probably imply the authorization of local financial regulators.		No regulation for securities crowdfunding yet exists.

Spain	Equity CF platforms are not treated as financial services providers, thus outside the supervision of CNMV and bank Of Spain. Lending models are regulated by the regime for corporations.	The lack of a specific regulation makes it very burdensome and inefficient to start a securities crowdfunding platform.	No regulation for securities crowdfunding yet exists.
UK	Equity CF platforms need an authorization by FCA, but some portals make use of exemptions. Lending platforms will need authorization from April 2014 onwards.	If investment is characterized as collective investment scheme, it cannot be promoted to retail investors. Threshold: €5mln per issuer within 12 months.	FCA will be soon releasing a regulation that will require from 2014:- Not to promote to the public the Special Purpose Investment Vehicles (SPVs). FCA Authorization for lending portals.

Each country is treating securities crowdfunding in a way that comports with an existing legal framework.

As the industry becomes more familiar, regulators will be better able to understand it and evaluate whether there is a need to create a specific regulation in order to facilitate its development or to protect investors. The challenge will be to harmonize the national crowdfunding regulations to facilitate a cross-border European crowdfunding market. The European Commission has encouraged its member states to look at what the others are doing and it is also launching a public consultation to frame European thoughts and opinion on the topic of crowdfunding.

III. Comparative Analysis of U.S. Crowdfunding Vehicles

TITLE TWO: Private Issuers Publicly Raising (PIPRs)

Reg D 506c exemption

Effective date: September 23, 2013

Filings: FORM D

No audited financials and no annual reporting

Costs: vary on banking fees

No offering limit

Must provide SEC verification that purchasers are accredited

Intermediary not required

ADVANTAGES

Can raise unlimited amount without Title III disclosure

TITLE III: Crowdfunding

4(a) (6) exemption

Effective date (est): June, 2014

Filings: FORM C, FORM C-U,

Audited financials; annual reporting for offerings in excess of $500,000

Costs: vary on banking fees

$1 million offering limit in each 12-month period

Limited general solicitation such as tombstone ads directing investors to funding portal

Must use funding portal or registered intermediary

ADVANTAGES

Unlimited number of investors; helps convert

burden; unlimited advertising
DISADVANTAGES
SEC verification requirements

Intrastate Crowdfunding ("LocaVesting")
Rule 147 offerings with few reporting requirements

Currently effective
Not costly
General solicitation permitted
ADVANTAGES
Can raise unlimited amount without Title III disclosure burden; ideal for retailers as it can bring communities together

customers into investors
DISADVANTAGES
$1M cap on annual raises; more reporting requirements than with Title II; disclosure requirements can be costly; 4(a)(6) investors must comply

Registered Crowdfunding

Non-exempt; must fully register and make notice filings with states
Currently effective
Costly
No offering limits; use of broker-dealer network
ADVANTAGES
Unlimited number of investors; prestige and public awareness; no resale restrictions

DISADVANTAGES

Limited to local capital market; non-accredited investors must comply with applicable limits

DISADVANTAGES

Costly

About the author

After getting a JD from Stanford Law School, a MA from the University of Chicago, a diploma from the University College London, and working as a reporter for The Wall Street Journal, Doug was a member of the California bar for 40 years, during which time he founded a series of law reporting services now owned by Thomson-Reuters. Doug specializes in debt and equity crowdfunding. He helps small business identify and solicit sources of private equity. Doug monitors a LinkedIn discussion group, State Securities Regulation, with 1500 members.

Connect with Douglas Slain:
LinkedIn: http://linkedin.com/in/douglasslain
Facebook: http://facebook.com/douglas.slain
Twitter: https://twitter.com/exemptofferings
Blog: http://www.privateplacementadvisors.com/apps/blog
Web site: http://privateplacementadvisors.com

www.ingramcontent.com/pod-product-compliance
Lightning Source LLC
Chambersburg PA
CBHW070736180526
45167CB00004B/1778